MONEY MATTERS

Saving

A Teen Guide to Saving for the Future

SARAH EASON

Published in 2026 by **Cheriton Children's Books**
1 Bank Drive West, Shrewsbury, Shropshire, SY3 9DJ, UK

First Edition

Author: Sarah Eason
Designer: Paul Myerscough
Editor: Kelly Short
Proofreader: Amy Strauss

Picture credits: Cover: Molibdenis Studio. Illustrations throughout by Molibdenis Studio. Inside: p4: Shutterstock/Kimberrywood, p5: Shutterstock/Simplylove, p6: Shutterstock/Fizkes, p7: Shutterstock/Kaspars Grinvalds, p8: Shutterstock/loreanto, p9: Shutterstock/Pics Five, p10l: Shutterstock/StoryTime Studio, p10r: Shutterstock/Zuumy, p13: Shutterstock/LightField Studios, p15: Shutterstock/Infinity Time, p17: Shutterstock/Antoniodiaz, p18: Shutterstock/Prostock Studio, p19: Shutterstock/BearFotos, pp20-21: Shutterstock/Perfect Wave, p22: Shutterstock/Lalaka, p24: Shutterstock/GretaW, p25: Shutterstock/Wk1003mike, p26: Shutterstock/Ground Picture, p27: Shutterstock/Ground Picture, p29: Shutterstock/GaudiLab, p30: Shutterstock/Prostock Studio, p31: Shutterstock/Miljan Zivkovic, pp32-33: Shutterstock/PrimeMockup, p34: Shutterstock/Hunter Bliss Images, p35: Shutterstock/Mauricio Graiki, p36: Shutterstock/Artem Varnitsin, p37: Shutterstock/Hriana, p38: Shutterstock/Inside Creative House, p40: Shutterstock/F8 Studio, p41: Shutterstock/Szefei, p42: Shutterstock/N Universe, p43: Shutterstock/Worradirek, pp44-45: Shutterstock/Mimagephotography.

Printed in China

Please visit our website,
www.cheritonchildrensbooks.com
to see more of our high-quality books.

Contents

CHAPTER 1

Why Money Matters

In the modern world, money directs almost everything we do. Money matters for everyone—and that includes teens. There is very little in anyone's life that is not affected by finances. We all depend on money for the things that we need and want.

From Teen to Adult

As a teen, those needs and wants will be simpler than they'll be when you become an adult. You'll need to provide for more "needs" as an adult, such as housing and food. You'll also need to pay bills. You'll want to put money aside for bigger "wants," such as a dream vacation or buying a new car. But the principles, or rules, of how you manage your money remain the same. Having the skills to manage your money will help with all aspects of your life, both now and in the future. The good news is that anyone can learn important money skills that will help them master their finances.

Money on My Mind

Many teens say that they worry about money, with around 54 percent stating that thinking about finances makes them anxious. They say they do not feel that they are taught enough about money at school. About 42 percent of teens say they have had no money-management classes in school, and about 73 percent say they would take courses in money management if they were available. There is a big gap in financial education for teens. This book will set out to address that lack of education and give teens the tools they need to feel confident about handling money and building their financial future.

Many teens want to develop financial skills, but are not sure how or where to learn them.

Mastering Money

People who lack financial skills often feel insecure about their future. The world we live in operates around money, and being able to manage money dictates much of how we live our lives. Not having the tools to navigate personal finances can make people feel underconfident and worried. Having money skills can relieve a lot of stress, because once you understand finances and how to manage them, you'll feel more in control of your life and your future.

Money Skills

With some simple financial skills, it is easy to get a grip on your money and feel in control of the sums going in and out. You can also develop those skills further, to help you make the most of your money. Some key financial skills include:

- Budgeting
- Saving
- Investing
- Earning
- Managing debt
- Managing credit
- Setting financial goals
- Understanding tax
- Learning about insurance
- Getting to grips with risk and return

Learning about Financial Literacy

If you are someone who hasn't spent a lot of time thinking about finances so far, this book is as much for you as it is for someone who is very financially literate. Being financially literate means understanding basic things to do with money. That includes budgeting, saving, debt, credit, and investing. It covers managing risk, planning for the future, and knowing about tax. It also means being able to recognize when something is too financially good to be true! Everyone needs to be financially literate these days to navigate modern life and get the most from their money.

People who are not financially literate are more likely to spend their money unwisely and find themselves in debt.

Making It Work for You

When you are financially literate, you can have a healthy and smart relationship with money. You understand how to make money work for you. With financial literacy you will not be alarmed or confused when people use the language of money. By the end of this book, we will have covered many key financial terms, and explained them, so you'll be well placed to handle any conversations about money in the future. Financial literacy gives you the tools you need to understand important information when you research money-related products.

The Key to Freedom

One of the greatest gifts that financial literacy will give you is a sense of control and freedom. When you are financially literate you understand the world of money and can make good decisions based on fact. You can choose how to spend your money. You can choose where to save your money. If you do decide to borrow money at any point, perhaps by using a credit card or getting a loan, you will be well equipped to understand the deals on offer and choose the best one for you. You will also be able to understand the language attached to lending, so you know exactly what you are getting yourself into.

You don't need to be great at math to master simple money skills, and money doesn't have to be complicated. In this book, we'll try to make it as simple and easy to understand as possible. We'll take the mystery out of money and the fear away from finances. We'll show you how money can be exciting, how it can give you freedom, and how it can help you shape your future.

Teens and Money

Surveys show that a lack of financial education is forcing teens to turn to unreliable sources to try to gain money-management skills. One-third of young adults use social media influencers as sources of information for financial literacy skills, with many teens relying on TikTok as the place they get their information.

Social media is probably not the best place to learn financial literacy skills!

Investing for the Future

In this book we will explore the skill of saving. The idea of saving part of your money may seem pointless to you at this stage of your life. After all, you likely feel that you have got years and years ahead of you to do all that "grown-up stuff." Saving can seem meaningless—until you discover how it can change your life right now. Saving is one of the most empowering of financial literacy tools. Put simply, saving now gives you choices in your future.

Saving Sets up Your Future

Saving means you have additional money for all the goals and dreams you have for your life. It gives you the chance to do things you could otherwise never do. Saving can help you achieve things that you want to do in the near future. For example, with spare money set aside, you can buy a new outfit or splurge on a birthday party in the year ahead. Saving can also help you bring about your longer-term aims for your future, for example, it could provide you with a deposit for your dream home when you are an adult.

Mastering Money

Savings also provide you with the means of grasping the chance to do something when an opportunity comes your way. For example, if at some point in the future you see a career that you'd really love to do, but it is different from the job you are currently in, you may want to stop that job and retrain. Having savings will mean you can take a break from work for a period of time while you get the skills you need. You might even decide to stop your job and set up a business. Savings will make that possible.

Having savings also helps you keep out of debt. If you find you need extra money for something, you can draw upon your savings. For example, if you are invited to go on a vacation with your friends, you can use some savings to help fund it.

Financial freedom is all about mastering financial literacy.

What Saving Can Do for You

And if you still need convincing, here are a few more reasons why you should take control of your financial future by saving:

- Having savings makes life less stressful—you know you have some money put away should you need it.
- Being able to save money helps you feel in control of your finances. That gives you a sense of independence and makes you feel good about yourself.

Taking Steps to Financial Freedom

We'll explore how to save now, while you are a teenager, and we'll also take a look at your future and the type of saving you'll need to work on as an adult. Along the way, we'll cover advice from financial experts, so that you can learn to save like a pro. So, are you ready to make money work for you? Then let's get started.

CHAPTER 2

The Basics of Saving

Put very simply, saving means creating wealth. It means using the money you have now to create even more money for your future. Imagine this as a forest. Some trees are already growing in that forest (your money). By taking some seeds from those trees and planting them, you are creating more trees (more money). Over time, those trees will grow bigger and bigger, and the forest will be full of large, healthy trees (even more money for you). You can decide before you plant those trees what you'd like to use them for in the future. You can also set aside some trees to see you through when life doesn't go to plan. That is the art of saving.

Setting Goals

The art of saving includes setting goals. Those goals are markers to aim for—they are the reasons why you are saving. Saving goals can be ones that you'd like to achieve soon: They are short-term goals. They can also be goals that may take you longer to achieve: They are long-term goals. An example of a short-term savings goal is setting aside enough money to be able to pay for some new clothes. A long-term goal might be saving enough money to take a vacation with your friends when you graduate high school.

Saving helps you build up your future wealth, and that helps you achieve your future dreams.

Budgeting and Saving: A Dream Team

Before we get too much further into savings, we need to talk about another financial literacy power tool: budgeting. Budgeting means planning your finances, and you will not be able to save without a budget. Budgeting is really quite simple. Here is how it works:

- **Figure out your income:** First check what money you get on a regular basis. This is your income. That money might come from your parents, as an allowance. You may earn it from doing a job, such as working in a café part time or helping out in a local store. Wherever it comes from, it is your income.
- **Figure out your expenditure:** Next, break down the money you get into what you spend it on. For example, that might include regular outgoings such as gym memberships, other subscriptions, and going out with your friends. Whatever it is, write it down. Once you have recorded everything, you can see exactly how much you have left for savings. Take a look at the diagram to the right to see how this might look.

Mastering Money

When you write down your income and expenditure, it might look like this. Below is the income and expenditure of an average teen. It shows money that is available for savings. You can model your own workings based on this, but obviously make sure the figures are correct for you!

Income:
Allowance: $80
Part-time job: $120

Total: $200

Expenditure:
Phone bill: $40
Transportation: $30
Clothes: $50

Total: $120

Making a Savings Plan

Now that we've learned about the value of savings, setting savings goals, and budgeting for them, let's look at how to create a savings plan. At a basic level, setting up a savings plan is fairly simple. This is how it works:

- **Set your goal:** Before you start saving, think about if you are saving for something specific and how much money you will need for it. That specific thing is your financial goal. Then figure out how much money you can afford to save on a regular basis. That is your regular savings figure. We'll talk more about how to set financial goals on the next few pages.
- **Create the plan:** Once you know how much you need to save, next look at how long it will take you to reach your goal if you regularly put aside your savings figure. Take a look at the diagram below to see how this might look.

Mastering Money

When you start to create your savings plan, it helps to write it all down. By writing it down, you are committing to it. You are then more likely to achieve it.

Vacation

Money needed: $750
Save per week: $75
Weeks to save: 10

On average, American teenagers save between $548 and $720 each year.

If I Don't Have a Goal, How Much Should I Save?

You don't need to have a goal to benefit from saving. Actually, saving a proportion of your income on a regular basis is very good financial practice. By saving regularly, you will have a "buffer" of money should you need it at some point. Life can throw you financial curve balls, so having a soft-landing pad of savings makes it easier to handle the knocks if they come your way. We'll talk a little more about the value of saving to help manage problems later in this chapter.

As a rule of thumb, many people try to set aside 10–20 percent of their income for savings. That is an achievable amount: It's not too much, but over time it can really add up to a large amount of money that could be very beneficial to you in the future.

SMART Goal Setting

When setting financial goals for your savings plan, you'll be much more likely to achieve them if you make them "SMART." The SMART stands for specific, measurable, achievable, relevant, and time-bound. SMART financial goals can be really useful when figuring out your savings plan because they make you focus on the detail of your goal. A SMART financial goal would work like this:

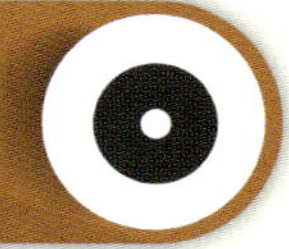

Specific:
I want to save $200 to buy a new camping tent.

Measurable:
I will save $10 per week.

Achievable:
I know $10 per week is a manageable amount—I will still have $15 dollars left to do with what I want.

Relevant:
Buying the new tent means a lot to me—I've got an exciting camping trip with my friends planned for this summer.

Time-bound:
I will have saved $200 in 20 weeks' time.

See It, Then Save It

Goal setting can be really fun and creative. One of the ways to make it exciting is to have financial milestones. People in finance often talk about having financial milestones. These are marker points in your financial journey through life. To set financial milestones, it helps to visualize how you would like your financial future to look in adulthood. You can then build a savings plan toward it. To do that, imagine yourself in the future in different time segments:

- **In 5 years' time:** My goal is...
- **In 10 years' time:** I will be...
- **In 15 years' time:** My goal is...
- **In 20 years' time:** I will have achieved...

By doing this activity, you'll be able to see what you would like your future to look like. You can then use the saving exercise on pages 12–13 to create a roadmap toward that future. You figure out how much money you will need to achieve each of your 5-year goals, then you figure out how much money you will need to save regularly to reach your goal in 5 years' time. If the amount you need to save is not realistic, you can just adjust your plan and make a goal a 10-year or 15-year goal instead. You can still achieve the goal; it just may take you a little longer to get to it.

Teens and Money

When you move from childhood into teenagerhood, your life tends to get more expensive. From ages 13 to 18, a teen's expenses begin to look more like adult ones. That includes going out with friends and maybe on dates, buying clothes, and likely paying for subscriptions and phone bills. This is why being able to budget and plan savings is so important at this life stage.

You need to be in control of your finances as you begin to take on more and more adult responsibilities. For example, if you move away from home, you'll need to pay rent and bills. You will need to earn money to cover those costs.

Get Financially Fit:

Save like a Pro

Expert Tips!

Financial experts have some great tips for helping people learn to save strategically. By having these techniques at hand, you'll be able to effectively set up your saving plan and change it as needed.

The 50/30/20 Rule

Financial experts advise people to split up their money into percentages: 50 percent for needs (the things you absolutely have to have, such as food and transportation), 30 percent for wants (the things that you'd like, such as a new bike), and 20 percent for savings. It's a good rule of thumb to follow for everyone, including teens.

When Income Changes, Change Your Plan

Teens often work unregularly. They may have a part-time job during school semester times, maybe just working at weekends only. During school breaks, such as during the long summer break, teens may work more. Having a savings plan that accommodates those changes is a good idea. If your earnings are likely to fluctuate, or go up and down, make sure your saving plan fluctuates too. For example, aim to save more during summer when your earnings will be greater, and be realistic about what you can save during school semester times.

Still SMART?

From time to time, it helps to check that your goals are still SMART. Are they still specific, measurable, achievable, relevant, and time-bound? If any part of that has shifted, you may need to reexamine the goals. Perhaps they don't feel achievable because you tried to save too much money too quickly. If that is the case, adjust your time frame and give yourself longer to save. Maybe a goal no longer feels relevant—perhaps it is not as important to you as it once was. In that case, you may need to change the specifics and put in place a new goal that you do care about. The beauty of SMART goals is that they give you a clear picture of what you are aiming for. If you find parts of those goals change, you just adapt your plan.

Saving for Setbacks

Experts encourage savers to build in an emergency plan. This is a pot of money that is allocated for when things go wrong, or life's financial curve balls. As an example of the value of savings in the face of financial curve balls, imagine you get a car at some point in the future. You might find that it breaks down and you need to pay for some expensive repairs. Without those repairs, you wouldn't be able to get your car back on the road. And if you need your car to get to a job or college, for example, that could put you in a pretty serious situation. Having some savings behind you means that you are prepared for financial setbacks, and will be able to get back on your feet again.

If your car breaks down in the future, having savings will make repair payments less stressful.

Be Committed

One of the keys to becoming great at saving is to stick at it! That may sound really simple and throwaway, but it's true. Persistence is your weapon when it comes to building wealth. If you can have the discipline to regularly save and not give up, you will find that your money builds and builds. And as it builds, it will be exciting to see and will encourage you to keep on going.

Don't Give Up

Learning to be a committed saver is a little like learning to ride a bike: You have to put in the practice and keep going. At first, you may find it tricky. It's all new and it can feel hard at times. That may make you feel like giving up, but don't! Just like learning to ride a bike, if you keep trying and practicing, it will get easier. Before you know it, you'll be saving as if you've done it all your life. And when you check in on those savings in the future and see how they've grown, you'll be really glad that you didn't give up.

Keep Checking In

Once you have your savings plan in place, and can see your money building up, it is a good idea to keep coming back to it and checking in on your original plan. Nothing in life stays the same, and that will apply to you and your financial goals. Flexibility is key to financial literacy skills. You may need to adapt and adjust your plans as life changes. For example, the original short-term goal that you set out to achieve might not feel as important when you near the date of achieving that goal. If you feel that you don't really care as much about buying that new piece of clothing or gadget, you don't have to buy it. You can instead change your plan, and maybe put the money toward another short-term goal, or a longer-term one.

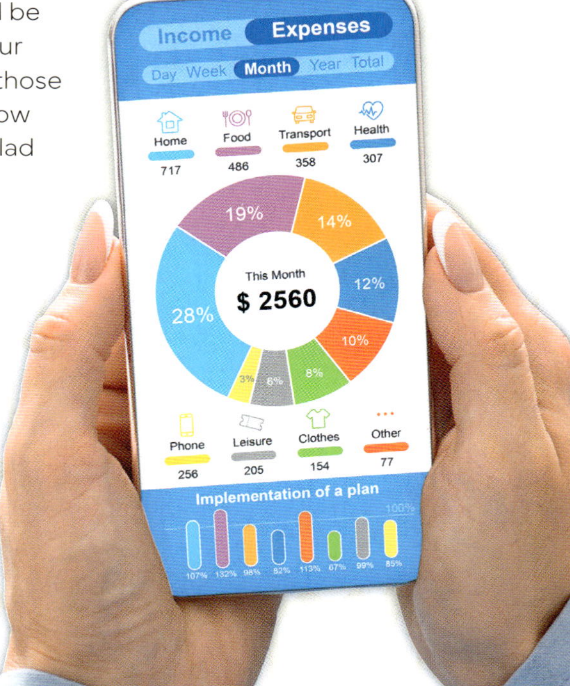

A money tracker app can be very helpful when trying to keep to a savings plan or budget.

Mastering Money

You can use goal tracker apps to help you keep on top of your savings plan and figure out if it is working for you. Apps like Greenlight and Copper Banking have specific goal-setting features. You can use them to help you set up your savings goals, monitor them, and put in place reminders to check in on your savings plan. The apps also provide lots of useful financial tips to help you grow your financial literacy skills.

If you decide that the thing you were saving for no longer excites you, don't spend your money on it! Instead, save it for something else you might want in the future.

Saving Made Easy

To remind you why saving should be one of your go-to financial literacy tools, take a look at this recap of chapter 2 and the basics of saving.

Saving Means Creating Wealth

We talked about viewing money as trees in a forest at the start of the chapter. The trees that exist are your money, and when you take seeds from them to plant new trees, you grow your money.

It's All about Setting Goals

Your financial goals are things that you are aiming to do with your money. They can be short- or long-term goals.

Budgeting Is Important

Budgeting means money that comes in (your income) and money that goes out (your expenditure). You need to know how to budget so that you can save. You look at your income and your expenditure, then see how much you have left to save.

You Need to Make a Plan

Without a plan, it is very difficult to save. A savings plan gives you a roadmap toward your goals: You can see how to get to them. To create a plan, you set your goals, figure out how much money you need for them, and how long it will take to save it. With that in place, you then know that you can reach your goals.

Everyone Should Save

Experts advise that people should try to save about 20 percent of their income, even if they do not have a specific goal in mind. All saving is beneficial. If you have savings, you have financial security and greater financial choices in the future.

Financial Goals Should Be SMART

Always try to make your financial goals SMART. That will help you to make sure they are specific, measurable, achievable, relevant, and time-bound. If you need to revisit the meaning of SMART goals, look again at page 14.

Set Financial Milestones

Having markers to aim for in the future, and a plan to get to them, makes it more likely that you'll achieve your goals. Try to put financial markers in place. You could start with a 5-year plan for example. You can revisit the information about financial markers on page 14.

Be Committed

Saving requires discipline and commitment, so don't give up. Keep saving and you'll be glad that you did when you see your pot of money growing.

Keep Checking In

Life changes, and your goals may change too. Remember to check in on your savings plan and adjust it if you need to.

CHAPTER 3

Where and Why to Save

Once you have decided how much you are going to save, the next step is to decide where you are going to save that money. This is where a savings account comes in. Many people have a regular account that they pay their money into, and a separate account for savings. That is for a number of reasons. First, putting your savings into an account separate from your regular money makes it less likely that you will spend it. You've set it aside for a reason. You're more likely to leave it in the savings account and less likely to spend it through carelessness. Second, keeping money in a savings account means that you can earn money from that money. This is called earning interest.

Earning by Saving

All accounts have interest attached to them. If you have money in the account, the bank or credit union that provides that account pays you money for keeping your money with them. The money they pay you is called interest. Interest is figured out based on rates that are set by the Federal Reserve. Banks and credit unions also look at interest rates offered by their competitors—other banks and credit unions—and set their interest rates so they are competitive.

Always look for a high-yield savings account when doing your research. This is an account that gives you a high rate of interest on your money.

The reason to put money into a savings account is because you will earn more interest than if you put your money in a regular bank account. That is because the rate of interest paid on a savings account is generally greater than the rate of interest paid on a regular account. So, your money will make even more money if you put it into an account with a higher rate of interest: the savings account.

Mastering Money

Another great reason to put your money in a savings account is compound interest. This means interest that grows and grows the longer you keep your money in a savings account. You start with a deposit of say $20 to open your high-yield savings account. A deposit is a sum of money that you pay into an account to start it off. Over time, you add to that $20 deposit. All the time too, you are earning interest on that money. That makes your $20 deposit, all the other money you have paid into the account, and the interest paid on top grow. Remember, you earn interest on the savings you put into the account and the interest paid into the account. So that means, the longer you leave your money in the account, and keep adding to it, the greater it will grow.

Imagine you start your savings plan with $100. This diagram shows how your money grows by an increasing amount each year thanks to compound interest.

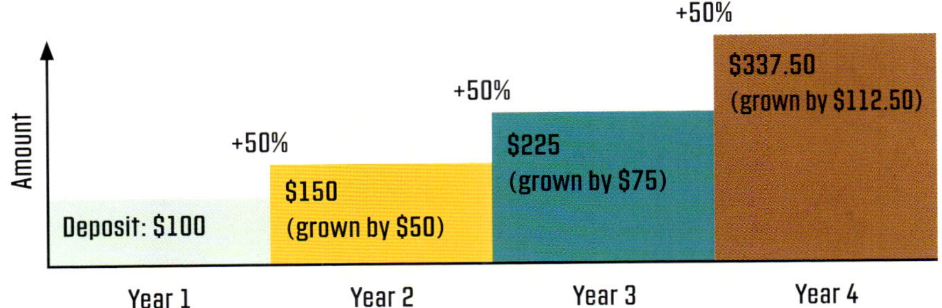

Compound interest works a little like a snowball effect, the longer it keeps rolling downhill and gathering more snow, the bigger it gets. So the longer you leave your money in the savings account, and keep paying money in, the more interest you earn and the bigger your financial snowball will be.

Keeping up with the Cost of Living

Have you heard of inflation? This is the increasing cost of living. The cost of living is what it costs to buy essential things such as food, heat a home, and put gasoline or diesel into a car to power it so you can travel to school or work. Over time, all these things become more and more expensive. If you compared the price of a pint of milk 20 years ago with a pint of milk today, it would be far more expensive now. In fact, 20 years ago, buying a pint of milk in the United States would have cost around 34 cents. But buying the same pint of milk today, costs around 51 cents. That's an increase of 50 percent—and that's a lot!

Beating Inflation

Inflation is another good reason to save money in a savings account, where it will gather interest. Imagine if you simply saved your money in a piggy bank. Week by week, or month by month, you put your money in. You might feel good to physically put those dollars in, but think about it: If you put 34 cents in a piggy bank, do you think that money will have grown by 50 percent in 20 years' time? No. But if you put the same amount of money in a savings account, and it grew at an interest rate of say 7 percent a year, for 20 years, it would be worth $1.37. And that's how you beat inflation by saving!

How to Keep Up

In a savings account, your money would have kept up with inflation, or the overall cost of living. It will have kept up because of compound interest. So, that is a major reason to put your money in a savings account. It will keep up with changes in prices in the long term, which means the things you want to buy in the future will be affordable if you want to use your savings to buy them.

Teens and Money

A recent study showed that 87 percent of teenagers believe saving money is important, and 20 percent said that they set yearly financial goals. However, only 42 percent of teens have any savings, and many teens do not have a bank account, which can make saving difficult.

It's safer to keep your money in a savings account than just putting it in a piggy bank—it's less likely to be stolen. You'll also need a pretty big piggy bank if you keep saving over a few years!

How Do You Find a Savings Account?

Now that you know about the value of savings accounts, you are probably wondering how you go about getting one. It is fairly straightforward to get a savings account, but the main thing is to find the best one for you. There are many different savings accounts available, so it pays to do plenty of research before opening one.

Getting the Best Deal

If you already have a bank account, your bank will likely be able to provide a savings account too. However, it pays to shop around before you commit to sticking with the account offered by your bank. Different savings account providers will offer different rates of interest, and different benefits. You may find that you can get a higher interest rate elsewhere. You can use comparison sites such as NerdWallet and Investopedia to help you do your research and find the best account.

Teens and Money

Some good and popular savings accounts for teens include Capital One Kids Savings Account, Alliant Credit Union Kids Savings Account, Current Teen Savings, and Bethpage Federal Credit Union Student Savings.

Always carefully compare interest rates before deciding on your savings account.

Be sure to check out a bank or credit union's mobile apps for keeping track of your account.

To inspire you to shop around for the very best interest rate on a savings account (and once again see the value of compound interest!), take a look at this example. If you managed to save $10,000 by the time you were 18 and put it into a savings account that had a rate of 7 percent interest, by the time you came to retire at age 65 for example, you would have a fund of about $240,000. You wouldn't need to put another dime in the account after the time you reach 18—your money would simply keep on growing without you needing to do a thing thanks to compound interest. Now imagine how that might look if you could secure a better rate than 7 percent. By finding the very best interest rate, you can earn money without needing to do a thing.

Good Offers for Teens

You can find savings accounts with banks and credit unions. Many offer teens good options with low fees and no minimum balance. That means they do not ask you to keep a certain amount of money in the account. Most offer savings accounts with mobile or online access too—few teens want to go into a bank or credit union to pay into or take money out of their account. And the good news for teens is that more and more banks and credit unions are phasing out instore services and instead expecting customers to do their banking online. That's another positive in the financial world for tech-savvy and finance-savvy teens.

Get Financially Fit:

Set It up like a Pro

Expert Tips!

Most financial experts agree that no matter how small an amount of money you save on a regular basis, it all adds up in the long term. There is great value in starting to save when you are young, even with just tiny sums of money. By starting to save early, you are setting up good habits for the rest of your financial life. And if you keep saving, that pot will get bigger (remember compound interest). Here are some more expert tips for great saving habits.

Check the Details

Always read the small print before choosing an account. These are all the finer details attached to the account. It may seem a bit boring to have to read through a lot of detail, and you may not understand it all. So, ask a parent or guardian to check through it all with you. In time, you'll come to understand more and more what financial terms and language mean. Look for accounts that do not have big monthly maintenance fees or hidden costs. These are charges that may be made to you for using the account, and can eat into your hard-earned money.

Being scammed is upsetting and shocking, and especially so when it means you lose your hard-earned money.

Be Ready to Move Your Money

If a term or deal on your savings account runs out, be ready to move your money. For example, some savings account providers may tempt new customers with a high interest rate for a set number of months, but once that term (or time) is over, the interest rate drops. If you open a savings account with a set term like this, put a note in your diary to review the account when it gets near to its term end, and research alternative savings accounts. If you find a better offer, move your money.

Invest Wisely and Watch Out for Scams!

Always do your research before investing any of your hard-earned money. There are plenty of scams and scammers out there, who are desperate to get their hands on your cash. They may persuade you that they have a great investment opportunity for you, which will give you eye-watering returns on your money. Remember the saying, "if it's too good to be true, it probably is!" If you stick to tried-and-trusted account providers, you know your money will be safe and you will not be scammed. If you have any concerns at all about putting your money in a savings plan, always talk to a trusted adult. They will be able to help and advise what to do.

What You Will Need to Open a Savings Account

You will need to have a parent or legal guardian as co-owner of the account if you are under 18 years old. So, be sure to ask a parent or guardian to help you research and choose the account. They will also be needed to fill in any paperwork to set up the account. Generally, a deposit of about $25 to $50 is needed to set up the account.

Proving Who You Are

You will also need proof of identity to set up an account. So too will your parent or guardian. Proof of identity means you can prove you are who you say you are, which can include:

- **For teens:** a birth certificate, social security card, or school ID
- **For parents/guardians:** photo ID such as a driving license or passport and proof of address, such as a utility bill (that can be a gas or electric bill, for example)
- **For both of you:** your Social Security Number

Seeing how much you have managed to save can inspire you to try other ways to save in the future.

In Person or Online?

Some banks will allow you to open an account online, but others will ask you to go into the bank in person to open an account. That is typical for minors, or people under the age of 18. If you do need to go into a bank to open the account, they will ask that the co-owner of the account goes in with you to set up the account.

Opening your first bank account is an exciting moment!

Mastering Money

Once you have opened a savings account, a great way to make sure you save regularly is to set up an automated transfer of money from your regular bank account to your savings account. This is called an automatic transfer. You can set your bank account to transfer, or send, a set amount of money into your savings account on a regular basis. So, for example, if you have a weekly allowance paid into your regular account, on the date that allowance is paid in you can set up to have a percentage of it paid into your savings account. If you are paid for a part-time job every month, you can do the same. You can set up to have a percentage of your earnings paid into your savings account.

By saving automatically, you don't need to think about paying money into your savings account. It just happens, so that's one less job for you. It's also surprisingly easy to accumulate a savings fund in this way. Try it. You might be surprised—and excited too—by how much you manage to save!

Saving Made Easy

In this chapter we've covered the value of saving, where to save your money, and how to go about setting up a savings account. Here is a quick, neat roundup. If you feel yourself struggling with the idea of setting up a savings account and how to go about it, take a look at these points below.

A Savings Account Will Pay You Back

Putting your money in a savings account over a regular account is good financial practice. A savings account will help your money grow because it has a much higher rate of interest. It is also absolutely the right place to keep your money —never stick it in a piggy bank or box at home. It is secure and safe in a savings account.

Remember the Value of Compound Interest

Compound interest really is a magical financial tool. Don't forget that if you save money into a savings account, you not only earn interest on that money, you earn interest on the interest too! It's like a snowball: The more that money grows in your account, the bigger your financial snowball gets. If you ever need to remind yourself of the value of compound interest, revisit the example on pages 26–27 of this book. How would you feel if you could have $240,000 in a savings account by the time you retire?

Don't Forget about Inflation

As time goes by, the cost of living goes up. That is the cost of food, gasoline, and other expenses that people have to find on a regular basis. If you put your money in a savings account, the interest on it will grow, and that will help you afford things in the future as prices continue to rise.

Shop Around

Always do your research before you open a savings account. Try to get the very best deal that you can—look for high-yield accounts that will give you a greater rate of interest on your money. There are some good deals out there for teens too, so make sure you investigate the very best option for you. Always ask a parent or guardian to help you with this if you find it difficult to do on your own. You will need them to help you set up the account, so it is good to have them on board from the outset.

Take What You Need to Open an Account

Once you have decided on a savings account, you will need to gather the paperwork to open it. Your parent/guardian will need to be a co-owner too, so will also need paperwork. You can revisit the information on pages 30–31 to remind you of documentation you will need to show.

CHAPTER 4

How to Save in the Future

If you talk to most adults, those who have saved some of their money will likely tell you it was a wise investment. It may have made it possible for them to achieve some of their life goals, big and small. And those who didn't save would likely tell you that they wish they had. They may regret not having saved some of their money, and not having learned the value of saving at an earlier stage of their lives. It may have held them back from achieving some of the things they wanted to do. The good news is that you are young. You have time to master the art of saving and make this financial tool your new best friend.

You Have the Tools

Learning how to save and invest your savings as a teen sets you up for a good relationship with your money as an adult. When you head toward adulthood, the financial milestones we talked about earlier become more real. Those milestones might include going to college or enrolling in a vocational training course once you leave school. They may include buying a car or saving a deposit for your first home. As you've now learned, by setting financial goals and planning your roadmap toward them, you can make your dreams a reality.

Big purchases like buying a car may feel like a pipe dream now, but you can achieve that dream if you save for it.

With financial literacy, as you enter your adult life, it will feel exciting rather than daunting to plan your future. You will have the tools to make it what you want.

Same Tools, Bigger Goals

Many of the topics we've discussed in previous chapters also apply to saving as an adult. They include budgeting, creating a savings plan, and having short- and long-term financial goals. The difference is that in your journey into adulthood, your goals may become bigger. You may plan to try to save more money to pay for bigger goals, such as taking a great vacation or buying a more expensive car. You will also begin to look more to your long-term future and focus on plans for your retirement, such as increasing your savings.

Mastering Money

When you have to save for something over a long period of time, when it comes to achieving that long-term financial goal, it feels really significant. It can feel great to have stuck with your savings plan and have committed to reaching your goal. And once you achieve your goal, such as buying your first car, it feels really great. That delay in buying something is called delayed gratification. It is a good experience to have because it teaches you to be patient about spending money, and to spend it wisely.

Whatever your future dreams are, having a financial plan will help you realize them.

Education After School

Another great reason to start saving now is that you may well want to go to college in the future. While that may seem a while away, it will come around sooner than you think, and having money saved will help pay for your time at college. Even if you choose not to go away to college, you may need money to help with training to kickstart your career. Or you may choose to go it alone and set up your own business. Either way, having some money set aside will help get you started and make it a lot easier to do whatever you choose to do once you finish school.

Plans to Consider

Here are some great savings plans that work well for college savings funds—if you have a conversation with your parents about financial plans for college, you could see if they have considered these options. They will likely be pleased that you have taken the time to research them and read this book, so share the knowledge!:

A 529 plan: This is one of the best and most popular ways to save for college. It is sponsored by state government to encourage people to save for their time at college. Many states offer tax deductions or credit, which is another great reason to set one up. These plans can be started with as little as $25.

One day, you may decide to start your own business—having savings will make that possible.

The downside of a Roth IRA that other relatives, such as grandparents, will not be able to contribute.

Savings bonds: These can be bought online from the US Department of the Treasury. They can be redeemed, or cashed in, to be used for paying for college education. They are also tax free. One thing to consider with savings bonds is that the interest on them is often quite low, so it may be worth considering higher-interest options.

Roth IRA: Most people think a Roth IRA is a pension-only savings fund (see page 43) but it can be used for other savings plans, such as a college fund. Contributions are tax free. The upside of this savings plan is that if you decide not to go to college in the end, the money in the account can be used for something else. If you try to use savings bonds for purposes other than education, for example, you will be taxed.

Teens and Money

As a teen, it is unlikely that you'll be able to save a significant amount of the money that you'll need for college. However, with your parents/guardians' help (or the help of other family members, such as grandparents), saving for this time of your life is achievable. If you haven't already had a conversation with your parents about college and savings plans, now is the time to do so. You may discover that they already have plans in place.

Get Financially Fit:

Plan like a Pro

Expert Tips!

College costs are not cheap. According to a recent study, the average yearly tuition fee in the college year 2024–2025 was between $43,505 for private colleges and $11,011 for public, in-state colleges. And costs are rising continually. That is why it is never too early to start saving for college, or any other further education you may want to undertake after you finish high school. If you start saving early, your savings will keep up with increases in costs.

Going to college is exciting and can be a great time of your life, but it is also expensive!

Start the Conversation

As we said on the previous pages, it's never too early to start talking to your parents about plans for college. You can offer to help contribute toward any savings plan too. For example, if your parents say they can contribute $25 a month toward the fund, you could offer to add $5. That way, they can see you are making a commitment to your financial future too. And with compound interest, your combined pot of money will get bigger.

Earn a Little Extra

Take a look at ways you could earn some more money to contribute to a college savings plan. It doesn't need to be a big commitment that takes you away from your studies. You could do some simple jobs, such as babysitting or dog walking. If you set aside the money you earn, it will all help build up your future funds.

Set Yourself a Savings Challenge

Do you like a challenge? If so, you could set yourself some fun financial goals. Start by aiming to save just $1 toward your college fund each month. Then month on month, try to increase that amount. For example, in month 1 you save $1, then in month 2 you save $1.50, in month 3 you save $2. It will be fun to see if you can hit your targets, and rewarding to see your savings increase. Maybe get your family involved too. If they can match your targets each time you hit them, imagine how much your savings might grow.

Master the Art of Budgeting

Just by tracking what you spend your money on, you can often find ways to cut back on your expenditure and save a little more. Try tracking your expenses for a month or so, then sit down with your findings. Can you see areas where you are spending money that you don't need to spend? Or are you spending it on things that you don't really want? If so, cut them out and instead put the money into your savings account. Imagine how you would rather spend that money—would you prefer to spend it on a couple of smoothies that you don't really need or put it toward your future education, which could help you get a great job?

Saving for a Car

When saving for a car, it is not just the car that you'll need to factor into your savings plans. You'll need to also consider all the many costs that come with a car. If buying a car becomes one of your long-term financial goals, you will need to build in the below costs as part of your savings plan:

Car insurance: This covers you for any healthcare costs in the event of an accident along with a certain amount of repairs to fix your car if it is damaged.

Fuel: You will need to factor in the costs of paying for gasoline or diesel to run your car.

Vehicle registration fee: This is an annual fee that allows you to drive a car on public roads.

Roadside assistance cover: This is a fee you pay to a company that will send out a mechanic if you break down. The mechanic will try to repair your car or get it to a garage where it can be fixed.

Car maintenance: You will need to keep your car roadworthy. That will mean keeping it serviced and paying for repairs if they are needed.

Saving for a Home

Buying a home is likely the biggest purchase that you will ever make. To buy a home you will need to save a deposit. This is a down payment on the property. The size of the down payment you will need to make will vary depending on the loan you get for your home. That loan is called a mortgage. Some mortgage lenders ask for as little as 3 percent of the property value. When you get closer to wanting to buy a home, you can research different mortgage options. You can also use money-research tools such as NerdWallet, which has a section that helps you figure out how much you can afford to spend on a house. You can then decide how much you need to save toward a deposit

You can use all of the information we covered in chapter 3 to help you find a savings plan that will work best for any future plans you may have.

Mastering Money

Remember too, unlike other things you may buy in the future, such as a home, a car never goes up in value. As soon as you buy a car, it's value starts to fall. That is called depreciation. For that reason, a car is something that you might need, to get to college or a job, for example. It is something that you might want. But unless you can afford to buy a supercar, it will not increase in value!

Saving for Retirement

Retirement is a long, long way off for you right now. But as with all savings plans, the sooner you start to think about them and put them into action, the more money you will have at the end of your plan. A pension will probably be the biggest long-term financial goal you will have. Some people have a personal pension plan, others have a pension plan with their employer, and some people have both.

Mastering Money

People who are smart with money start a pension plan as soon as they possibly can. Once you start working, one of the very best places to save your money is in a pension plan. That is because you get tax relief on your pension (see opposite). Tax relief is money that you are not required to pay tax on.

A pension fund grows over time, so the earlier you start one, the greater your savings will be when the time comes for you to retire.

Personal Pension Plans

There are different options for personal retirement savings plans. These are called Individual Retirement Arrangements (IRAs). Many people choose from two different types: traditional IRAs and Roth IRAs. Both have benefits.

Traditional IRAs allow you to put in pre-tax dollars. That is money you have earned but will not be taxed on. That lowers the overall tax you have to pay on your income. That means you keep more of your hard-earned money in the short term. However, you will have to pay tax on your pension when you withdraw it, or take it, when you retire. Roth IRAs work in a different way. You pay in dollars after your earnings have been taxed, but when you come to withdraw your money on retirement it is tax free. That means you will not need to pay any tax on your retirement income in the future.

Employer Pension Plans

If you are employed in the future rather than self-employed, look out for any retirement plan that is offered by your employer. These are often 401(k) retirement plans. These plans allow you to make yearly contributions up to a limit of about $23,000 if you are younger than 50 years old. When you are 50 years or older, you can add another $7,500.

These plans are a really great way to save for your pension because your employer will contribute toward them. You can often put a large sum of money into such a plan (if you can afford it) and your employer may match that sum with their own contribution. That means you could save a significant amount of money into your pension year on year. And remember compound interest? The more you save, the more interest you will earn. Your career will likely last more than 40 years, so the amount you will have saved by the time you get to retirement could be sizeable.

Saving Made Easy

You've reached the end of the book and you'll have gained some powerful financial literacy skills along the way. They include the incredible power of saving and what it can do for your future. You've also discovered how to research where to best save your money and invest it wisely. You'll have learned why money matters, how to make it work for you, and have the skills to make your financial future whatever you want it to be. Let's recap everything we've covered in this chapter.

You've Got the Skills to Save

Saving as an adult is no different to saving as a teen. You are simply trying to save for bigger financial goals. All the principles are the same. The financial literacy skills you've learned by reading this book will set you up for a life of successful saving as an adult.

Just remember, saving is about:

- **Commitment:** You need to stick to a savings plan.
- **Setting goals:** When you have goals, you can plan a financial path to them.
- **Building future wealth:** The earlier you start saving the more wealth you'll accumulate in time.

Savings Plans for College

There are plenty of ways that you can save for college, and both you and your family can contribute toward them. Have that conversation about college funds as soon as you can and don't forget to check out the plan options on pages 36–37.

Cars and Homes

Buying your first car can feel amazing, but you need to be sure you have factored in the costs that come with it. Don't forget to make all the costs of car ownership part of your savings plan. If you feel yourself getting carried away by the idea of owning a car, check the list on page 40. You'll see everything you need to build in to your savings plan. It can still be exciting to plan for a car, just make sure you have everything covered in your financial planning.

Probably one of the most exciting purchases you will ever make is your first home, if you choose to be a homeowner. Saving toward that goal will likely be a long-term journey, but if you put your savings plan in place early enough, you can easily reach your end point.

Saving for Later Life

A pension plan is not boring! When you reach retirement, you'll likely want to do many fun and exciting things, and having a pension will mean that you can do them. It's never too soon to start saving for retirement, so as soon as you start work, remember to set up your plan.

All of the information we've covered in this book will help you navigate the world of savings and empower you to make the very most of your money now and in the future. Keep saving, keep investing in your future, and build the wealth that will help you achieve your dreams.

Glossary

adapt to change or adjust to new situations or conditions
afford to be able to pay for something without causing financial problems
allocated set aside for a specific purpose such as savings or expenses
anxious feeling worried or nervous, often about money or future costs
automated transfer a scheduled movement of money between bank accounts such as paying bills
automatically happening by itself without manual action
bank a financial institution that holds money and provides financial services
benefit a positive outcome or advantage such as earning interest on savings
budgeting planning how to spend and save money wisely
committed dedicated to a decision, such as regularly saving money
contributions money given toward savings investments or charity
credit borrowed money that must be paid back, usually with interest
credit card a card that allows purchases on borrowed money with payments due later
credit union a nonprofit financial institution that offers banking services to members
debt money owed to others, such as loans or unpaid bills
deposit money placed into a bank account for safekeeping
dictates decides or controls how something should be done
empowering giving confidence
federal reserve the central banking system
finances a person's money, savings, debts, and overall financial situation
gratification feeling satisfied, especially after achieving a financial goal
habits regular behaviors, such as saving money or tracking expenses
insecure feeling uncertain or unsafe
insurance a protection plan that covers costs in emergencies
interest rates the percentage charged on loans or earned on savings
investing using money to make it grow in value
legal guardian a person legally responsible for someone under 18
loan money borrowed that must be paid back over time
percentages parts of a whole often used in financial calculations
persistence continuing to do something even when it is difficult
retire to stop working
retrain to learn new skills for a different job or career
risk and return the potential loss and possible gain from an investment
scammers people who try to trick people
scams fake schemes meant to steal money or personal information
significant large or important
Social Security Number a unique US government ID used for work and benefits
strategically planning wisely
subscriptions recurring payments for services like streaming or magazines
tax money paid to the government to fund public services
wealth money, assets, and resources a person owns

Find Out More

Books

Explore other *Money Matters* books to find out more about how to make your money work for you:

Eason, Sarah. *Budgeting* (Money Matters). Cheriton Children's Books, 2026.

Sanderson, Jennifer. *Jobs and Taxes* (Money Matters). Cheriton Children's Books, 2026.

Sanderson, Jennifer. *Loans and Credit* (Money Matters). Cheriton Children's Books, 2026.

Websites

Take a look at this article at CNBC about savings accounts for teens:
www.cnbc.com/select/best-savings-accounts-for-kids

Forbes has lots of information on choosing the best savings account and how to go about it. Take a look at:
www.forbes.com/advisor/banking/savings/best-savings-accounts-for-kids

Investopedia is another great site to visit to research savings accounts:
www.investopedia.com/the-best-savings-accounts-for-kids-8783880

Visit NerdWallet to find out more about opening a savings account and to research different options. This page on their site shows the accounts they think are good, why they like them, and what you will need to set up an account:
www.nerdwallet.com/best/banking/kids-savings-accounts

Publisher's note to educators and parents:
All the websites featured above have been carefully reviewed to ensure that they are suitable for students. However, many websites change often, and we cannot guarantee that a site's future contents will continue to meet our high standards of educational value. Please be advised that students should be closely monitored whenever they access the Internet.

Index

About the Author

Sarah Eason has written a number of books for teens and young adults. She hopes that this book is a great way for them to spring into financial literacy and build skills that will see them through their teenage years and into adulthood with confidence.